Coping With BPD

The Ultimate Guide on How to Cope with Borderline personality Disorder

Tom Pete

Table of Contents

Chapter 1

Understanding Borderline Personality Disorder

This is how people, including mental health professionals, describe those with Borderline Personality Disorder (BPD). But given what a person with BPD has to deal with daily, these labels are not fair. Individuals suffering from Borderline Personality Disorder are akin to those who have third-degree burns over 90% of their body. Without emotional skin, they feel agony at the slightest touch or movement. This is how BPD specialist Marsha Linehan describes this deeply misunderstood mental illness.

This badly burned **emotional skin** means that people living with BPD do not have the ability to regulate their emotions, behaviors, and thoughts. In fact, "Dysregulation Disorder" would be a more accurate and less stigmatizing name for this illness. Like other personality disorders, BPD is a long-term pattern of behavior that begins in adolescence or early adulthood. But what makes BPD unique from other personality disorders is the emotional, interpersonal, personal, behavioral, and cognitive dysregulation.

Relationships can profoundly affect the self-image, behavior, and ability to function of a person with BPD. The possibility of facing separation or rejection can lead to self-destructive behaviors, self-harm, or suicidal thoughts. The lack of meaningful and supportive relationships damages their self-image. Sometimes they may feel as if they do not exist at all.

When starting a new relationship, a person with BPD may demand to spend a lot of time with their partner. They share their most intimate details right away to quickly create a meaningful relationship. At first, they will show immense love and admiration for their partner. But if they feel that their lover doesn't care enough, doesn't give them enough, or doesn't appreciate them enough in return, they will quickly move on to feelings of anger and hatred.

In this space of devaluing his or her partner, a person with BPD may display extreme or inappropriate anger, followed by intense feelings of shame and guilt. These feelings often contribute to a self-image of being evil or perverse. Possibly for this reason, people with borderline personality disorder are among the population at highest risk for suicide (along with anorexia nervosa, depression, and bipolar disorder). Completed suicide occurs in 10% of people with BPD, and 75% of people with BPD have cut, burned, beaten, or self-harmed. These self-destructive behaviors are often a response to threats of separation or rejection, but may also occur to reassert the ability to feel.

Definition of BPD

If you have borderline personality disorder (BPD), you probably feel like you're on a roller coaster, and not just because of the instability of your emotions or relationships, but also because of the oscillating sense of who you are. Your self-image, your goals, and even your likes and dislikes can often change in confusing and unclear ways.

BPD sufferers are frequently exceedingly sensitive. It is said by some that they have an exposed nerve ending. Little things can trigger intense reactions. And once upset, they find it difficult to calm down. It's easy to understand how this emotional volatility and inability to calm down leads to disturbed relationships and impulsive, even reckless behavior.

When you are engulfed in overflowing emotions, you can't think clearly or keep your feet on the ground. You may say offensive things or act in dangerous or inappropriate ways, which makes you feel guilty or ashamed later. It's a painful cycle that may seem impossible to escape. But it's not. There are effective BPD treatments and coping techniques that can help you feel better and regain control of your thoughts, feelings, and actions.

The majority of mental health experts think that a mix of hereditary or internal biological characteristics and external environmental influences, like traumatic childhood experiences, is what causes borderline personality disorder (BPD).

There are many complex things going on in the BPD brain, and researchers are still trying to understand what it all means. However, in essence, your brain is always on high alert if you have BPD. You experience things more anxiously and fearfully than other people do. Your fight-or-flight switch is easily activated and, once activated, it robs your rational brain, triggering primitive survival instincts that are not always appropriate for the situation at hand.

It could appear like nothing can be done. What can you do, after all, if your brain is different? However, the truth is that your brain is changeable. You are building new neural pathways each time you use a new self-calming method or coping mechanism. Certain therapies, including mindfulness meditation, even promote the growth of brain matter. Additionally, these pathways get stronger and more automatic the more you train. Thus, persevere. It's possible to alter your thoughts, feelings, and behaviors with patience and commitment.

When psychologists talk about "personality," they mean the patterns of thinking, feeling, and behaving that make each of us unique. No one acts exactly the same all the time, but we tend to interact and relate to the world in a fairly consistent way. That's why people are often described as "shy," "outgoing," "meticulous," "funny," etc. These are elements of personality.

Because personality is so intrinsically linked to identity, the term "personality disorder" can lead one to think that there is something fundamentally wrong with who one is. But a personality disorder is not a judgment of character. In clinical terms, "personality disorder" means that your pattern of relating to the world is significantly different from the norm in other words, you don't act as most people expect. This causes you constant problems in many areas of your life, such as your relationships, your career, and your feelings about yourself and others. But more importantly, these patterns can be changed.

Recognizing the Signs and Symptoms

Signs and symptoms of borderline personality disorder usually appear in late adolescence or early adulthood. A disturbing event or stressful experience may trigger symptoms or aggravate them. Over time, symptoms usually diminish and may disappear completely.

BPD symptoms can range from manageable to very severe and may include any combination of the following factors:

Fear of abandonment: It is common for people with BPD to feel uncomfortable when they are alone. When people with BPD feel that they are being abandoned or neglected, they experience intense fear or anger. They may track the whereabouts of loved ones or prevent them from leaving. Or they may push people away before getting too close to avoid rejection.

Unstable and intense relationships: People with BPD find it difficult to maintain healthy personal relationships because they tend to change their opinions of others abruptly and drastically. They can quickly go from idealizing others to devaluing them, and vice versa. BDP individual marriages, friendships, and relationships with family members are often unstable and chaotic.

Unstable sense of self: Individuals with BPD frequently experience shame, guilt, and a distorted or confusing sense of who they are. They also frequently perceive themselves as "bad". They may also abruptly and drastically change their self-image, for example, by suddenly changing their goals, opinions, careers, or friends. They frequently undermine their own advancement as well. For instance, they might purposefully fail an exam, sabotage relationships, or lose their job.

Rapid mood swings: People with BPD may experience sudden changes in the way they feel about others, themselves, and the world around them. Irrational emotions, such as uncontrollable anger, fear, anxiety, hatred, sadness, and love, change frequently and suddenly. These alterations seldom persist longer than a few days and typically just last a few hours.

Impulsive and risky behavior: BPD sufferers frequently engage in episodes of reckless driving, fighting, substance misuse, binge eating, and/or risky sexual activity.

Suicidal ideation or behavior: People suffering from this personality disorder may burn, cut, or make threats to harm themselves. They may also have suicidal thoughts. They may also have suicidal thoughts. These self-destructive acts are often triggered by rejection, possible abandonment, or disappointment by a caregiver or lover.

Persistent feelings of emptiness: Many people with BPD feel sad, bored, dissatisfied, or "empty". Self-loathing and feelings of worthlessness are also prevalent.

Anger control problems: People with BPD have difficulty controlling their anger and often become intensely angry. They might use bitterness, sarcasm, or outbursts of rage to vent their rage. Guilt and shame frequently accompany these incidents.

Momentary paranoid thoughts: Severe stress, typically related to a fear of being abandoned, can set off dissociative episodes, paranoid thoughts, and occasionally hallucinations. These are transient symptoms that are typically not severe enough to be classified as a distinct illness.

Not every individual with borderline personality disorder exhibits every one of these signs. Every individual has different symptoms in terms of intensity, frequency, and length.

Chapter 2

Navigating the Emotional Roller Coaster

A large number of individuals with borderline personality disorder (BPD) struggle to control their strong emotions. One of the main symptoms of borderline personality disorder (BPD) is emotional dysregulation, which also explains other aspects of the condition like erratic relationships, risk-taking or impulsive conduct, and mental changes brought on by stress.

Another component of the BPD diagnostic criteria is emotional instability. Emotion regulation is a rather complex combination of ways in which a person relates to emotional experiences and acts accordingly. This includes the ability to behave appropriately when distressed, identify, understand, and accept emotional experiences, and utilize healthy strategies to manage uncomfortable emotions.

People with emotional regulation skills are able to control impulses to engage in impulsive behaviors, such as self-injury, reckless behavior, or physical aggression during periods of emotional stress. Emotional regulation skills are developed during childhood. As we grow up, we learn strategies that help us to understand how we feel and to calm down when we are distressed. ***Several factors can negatively influence this process, among them are:***

- *Childhood stress or trauma*
- *Punitive or controlling parents*
- *Differences in brain structure*
- *Lack of secure attachment to parents*
- *Emotion regulation versus dysregulation*

While emotion regulation allows us to overcome setbacks, a person with emotional dysregulation will have difficulty understanding their feelings and reacting to them in a healthy way. This is critical in BPD, as people with this disorder often experience significant distress in emotional situations.

Our ability to regulate emotions plays an important role in how we respond to events in our lives. For example, if a person with emotional regulation skills experiences a breakup, he or she is likely to feel sad and even a little depressed, but will be able to control his or her emotions and continue with daily routines.

However, if a person with BPD experiences the same situation, they may become depressed to the point of not being able to function. They may cope with the situation with destructive or violent behavior, or impulsive activities such as promiscuity.

BPD and emotional problems

People with BPD show a number of symptoms related to their ability to regulate their emotions. Each of these can cause major problems in daily life, leading to anxiety and depression, making it difficult to maintain stable relationships, or causing problems at work. People with BPD may also resort to impulsive, self-destructive, or even self-aggressive behaviors as a way of coping with emotional dysregulation.

Rapid mood swings and irritability

People with borderline personality disorder have difficulty controlling their moods and expressing their emotions, resulting in anxiety and irritability. Mood swings can be intense and rapid. These feelings of anxiety and irritability can interfere with their normal activities, such as working at a job or even taking care of themselves. Other people may find it difficult to be around you during these episodes for a variety of reasons, jeopardizing your relationships.

Emotional sensitivity may drive the mood swings and irritability displayed by people with BPD. A person with this disorder is likely to be more emotionally sensitive in general, leading him or her to react quickly and intensely to situations that come up.

Difficulty controlling anger

Severe mood swings are accompanied by sudden outbursts of rage. Even minor inconveniences can trigger anger in people with BPD, which can lead to destructive or violent behavior, including self-injury.

Emotion dysregulation appears to be closely related to anger management problems. Relationship intensity and stability may also play an important role in this context, as people with unstable and chaotic relationships may be more prone to aggressive behavior.

Feeling of emptiness

People with BPD often have a chronic sense of emptiness. Although the origin of this feeling is not entirely clear, it may be related to an insecure self-image. A person with BPD may have difficulty maintaining a firm grasp of his or her identity and may feel disconnected from self and others.

It can also cause loneliness, as the person suffering from chronic emptiness may feel disconnected from others and have difficulty maintaining friendships. This isolation can make it difficult to regulate emotions, which can initiate a vicious cycle that exacerbates feelings of distress and emptiness.

3 keys to coping with BPD:

- *Calm the emotional storm*
- *Learn to control impulsivity and tolerate distress.*
- *Improve your interpersonal skills*

Calming the Emotional Storm

As a person with BPD, you've probably spent a lot of time struggling with your impulses and emotions, so acceptance can be a difficult thing to grasp. But accepting your emotions doesn't mean condoning them or resigning yourself to suffering. It just means that you stop fighting, avoiding, suppressing, or denying what you're feeling. Giving yourself permission to have those feelings can take a lot of power away from them.

Just try to experience your feelings without judging or criticizing them. Give up on the past and the future and concentrate only on the here and now. Mindfulness techniques can be very effective here. Start by observing your emotions from the outside. Observe how they come and go, it can be helpful to think of them as waves. Pay attention to the bodily experiences that correspond with your feelings. Tell yourself that you accept what you are feeling right now. Remember that just because you feel something does not mean it is a reality.

Engage in activities that arouse your senses
Stimulating the senses is one of the quickest and easiest ways to calm down quickly. You will need to experiment to find out what sensory stimulation works best for you. You will also need different strategies for different moods. What can help you when you're angry or agitated is very different from what can help you when you're numb or depressed. ***Here are some suggestions:***

Touch: If you don't feel enough, try running hot or cold, but not boiling water, over your hands; hold a piece of ice; or grip an object or the edge of a piece of furniture as firmly as possible. If you feel too much and need to calm down, try taking a hot bath or shower, cuddling under the covers, or snuggling with a pet.

Taste: If you feel empty and numb, try sucking on strong-tasting candy or treats, or slowly eat something intensely flavored, such as chips with salt and vinegar. Try something calming, like soup or hot tea, if you want to relax.

Sniff: Light a candle, smell the flowers, try aromatherapy, spritz on your favorite perfume, or prepare something in the kitchen that smells good. You may find that you react better to strong smells, such as citrus, spices, and incense.

Sight: Pay close attention to a visual that grabs your interest. It can be something from your immediate surroundings, a fantastic view, a beautiful flower arrangement, a favorite painting or photograph, or something you visualize in your imagination.

Sound: Try listening to loud music, ringing a bell, or blowing a whistle when you need a jolt. To calm yourself, play soft music or listen to soothing sounds of nature, such as wind, birds, or the sea. A stereo works well if you can't hear the actual sound.

Reduce your emotional vulnerability: You are more likely to feel negative emotions when you are exhausted and stressed. That's why it's so important to take care of your physical and mental well-being.

Take care of yourself: Avoid mood-altering drugs, eat a balanced and nutritious diet, get plenty of sleep, exercise regularly, minimize stress and practice relaxation techniques

Learn To Control Impulsivity and Tolerate Stress

The relaxation techniques mentioned above can help you relax when you begin to feel overwhelmed by stress. But what to do when you feel overwhelmed by difficult feelings? This is where the impulsivity of BPD comes in. In the heat of the moment, you're so desperate to find relief that you'll do anything, including things you know you shouldn't do, such as cutting, reckless sex, dangerous driving, and binge drinking. You can even believe that you are powerless.

Moving from not controlling your behavior to controlling it
It is important to recognize that these impulsive behaviors have a purpose.
They are coping mechanisms for distress. They make us feel better, if only
for a moment, but the long-term costs are very high.

Regaining control of behavior starts with learning to tolerate distress. This
is the key to changing the destructive patterns of BPD. The ability to
tolerate distress will help you pause when you feel like acting out. Instead
of reacting to difficult emotions with self-destructive behaviors, you will
learn to cope by maintaining control of the experience.

A stabilization exercise to help you pause and regain control
When the fight or flight response is triggered, there is no way to "think
you're calm." Instead of focusing on your thoughts, focus on what you feel
in your body. The following stabilization exercise is a simple and quick way
to curb impulsivity, calm yourself, and regain control. It can make a big
difference in just a few minutes. Locate a peaceful area and take a comfy
seat.

Concentrate on what you feel in your body. Feel the surface you are sitting
on. Feel your feet on the floor. Feel your hands in your lap.
Concentrate on your breathing, taking slow, deep breaths. Inhale slowly.
Pause for a count of three. Then exhale slowly, pausing again for a count
of three. Keep doing this for several minutes.
In an emergency, distract yourself

If your attempts to calm down don't work and you begin to feel
overwhelmed by destructive urges, distracting yourself can help. All you
need is something to capture your attention long enough for the negative
impulse to go away. Anything that captures your attention can work, but
distraction is most effective when the activity is also calming. In addition
to the sensory strategies mentioned above, ***here are some things you can try:***

Watching TV: Choose something that's the opposite of how you feel: a
sitcom if you're sad, or something relaxing if you're angry or agitated.

Do something that you enjoy and, keeps you busy: It can be anything: gardening, painting, playing an instrument, knitting, reading a book, playing a computer game, or doing Sudoku or word search.

Get busy with work: You can also distract yourself with chores and errands: cleaning the house, gardening, shopping, caring for your pet, or doing the dishes.

Stay active: Vigorous physical exercise is a healthy way to release adrenaline and release tension. If you're feeling stressed, you can try more relaxing activities, such as yoga or a walk around the neighborhood.

Call a friend: Talking to someone you trust can be a quick and very effective way to distract yourself, feel better, and gain perspective.

Improve Your Interpersonal Skills

If you have borderline personality disorder, you have probably found it difficult to maintain stable and satisfying relationships with boyfriends, co-workers, and friends. This is because you find it difficult to distance yourself and see things from the perspective of others. You tend to misinterpret others' thoughts and feelings to misunderstand how others see you, and to ignore how your behavior affects them. It's not that you don't care, but you have a huge blind hole when it comes to other people. The first step is to acknowledge your interpersonal blind spot. Once you stop blaming others, you can start taking steps to improve your relationships and social skills.

Check your assumptions
When you are affected by stress and negativity, as people with BPD often are, it is easy to misinterpret the intentions of others. If you are aware of this tendency, check your assumptions. Remember that you cannot read minds. Instead of jumping to conclusions (usually negative), consider alternative motivations. For example, suppose your partner has been

abrupt with you on the phone and now you feel insecure and fear that he or she has lost interest in you. Before acting on these feelings

Stop to consider the possibilities

Perhaps your partner is under pressure at work. Maybe he's having a stressful day. Maybe he hasn't had his coffee yet. His actions could have a lot of different reasons.

Ask him to clarify his intentions

One of the easiest ways to check your assumptions is to ask the other person what they are thinking or feeling. Check what he meant by his words or actions. Instead of asking in an accusatory way, try a softer approach: "I may be wrong, but it seems to me that..." or "I may be being overly sensitive, but I have a feeling that...".

Put an end to the projection

Do you often project your negative feelings onto others? When you're unhappy with yourself, do you attack other people? Do you feel comments or constructive criticism as a personal attack? If so, you may have a projection problem.

To combat projection, you'll have to learn to step on the brakes, just as you did to curb your impulsive behavior. Be mindful of your feelings and your body's physical experiences. Take note of signs of stress, such as rapid heartbeat, muscle tension, sweating, nausea, or dizziness. When you feel this way, you are likely to lash out and say something you will regret later. Pause and take slow, deep breaths, and then ask yourself the following three questions:

- *Am I angry with myself?*
- *Do I feel ashamed or afraid?*
- *Am I worried about being abandoned?*

If the answer is yes, pause the conversation. Tell the other person that you are feeling emotional and would like time to think before continuing.

Take responsibility for your role

Ultimately, you should own up to the part you play in your relationships. Consider the ways in which your actions may exacerbate issues. How do your actions and words affect the feelings of those you love? Do you let yourself be tempted to judge someone else positively or negatively? You will start to see improvements in the caliber of your relationships if you try to put yourself in other people's positions, extend an open mind, and lower your defensiveness.

Chapter 3

Building a Foundation for Coping

Psychotherapy, or talk therapy, is the primary treatment for borderline personality disorder (BPD). Several types of therapy can benefit people with BPD, and each type takes a different approach.

Talk therapy teaches people vital skills to control their thoughts and emotions. There are many types of therapy, and each has its own goals and methods. Before locating a therapy that works for them, a person may need to attempt a few different kinds.

Certain drugs may also be helpful for an individual with BPD. The Food and Drug Administration (FDA) has not yet approved a medication to specifically treat BPD, but mood-stabilizing drugs, antidepressants, or antipsychotics may help with anxiety, hostility, or depression.

Types of Therapy

A person may attend therapy for BPD individually or as part of a group session guided by a therapist. In addition, some therapists offer telephone contact between sessions.

People with BPD can benefit from group sessions by learning effective self-expression and strengthening their interpersonal connections.

DBT
DBT helps people manage challenging emotions through both individual and group therapy. Teaching techniques that improve mindfulness, aid in tolerating discomfort, control emotions, and manage relationships is the aim.

Dr. Marsha Linehan developed DBT specifically for people with BPD who are thinking about taking their own lives. Though it places greater emphasis on relationships and emotions, it is comparable to cognitive behavioral therapy. Weekly individual therapy sessions, group coaching sessions, homework assignments, and phone assistance from the therapist when necessary are all typical components of DBT.

A 2016 review found that DBT is the only treatment for BPD that has empirical support. Previous research attests to the fact that DBT keeps patients in treatment longer and lowers hospitalizations and self-harm.

MBT
The goal of MBT is to help people with BPD understand their own and others' mental states. The basic hypothesis of BPD is that its primary symptom, trouble comprehending others, inhibits the development of solid relationships.

MBT teaches people that they may be misinterpreting the thoughts, feelings, and emotions of others. It encourages them to take a step back and evaluate whether their thoughts and beliefs are helpful and realistic. A 2019 review found evidence that MBT can be as effective as other therapies for BPD. The researchers do concede, though, that a large number of the studies they examined were of low quality and may have been biased. More research is required to fully comprehend the potential advantages of MBT.

Mindfulness Methods

Mindfulness methods can be used when necessary to help reduce the intensity of situations. Techniques such as the Five Things, mindful walking, observing your thoughts, and practicing positive affirmations can be used more regularly to achieve subtle, long-term changes in emotional management. Treat yourself with kindness if you fail to apply these strategies. Self-criticism is a harmful strategy that will exacerbate existing symptoms.

Here are four mindfulness techniques for BPD:

Five things - Grounding

When you feel overwhelmed by emotions or thoughts, stop for a moment to focus on your senses. This method works wonders for easing tension. If you are feeling very reactive, anxious, angry, or experiencing other intense emotions, use the Five Things technique to stabilize yourself.

Identifying the need to use this technique can be difficult when emotions overwhelm you. Find a way to remind yourself of this exercise, for example by putting a note on your cell phone or in a place where you can see it regularly.

Here are the steps of the Five Things technique:

- *Find five things you can see. Name them.*
- *Find four things you can touch. Touch them.*
- *Find three things you can hear. Listen to them.*
- *Find two things you can smell. Smell them.*
- *Find something you can taste. Taste it.*

Mindful Walking

Sometimes creating physical space can be a more tangible way to address emotional situations. Start by taking a deep breath and objectively observing your body, allowing it to exist only as a collection of muscles, organs, and tissues. Think about which muscles you are going to activate to take the first step - will you start with your right leg or your left? When you are ready, take an intentional step.

Start slowly and notice the details during the meditation. Feel how your clothes move and how your feet feel in your shoes. Notice also your breathing as you walk. Practice following your body and be aware of everything that happens with each movement. Pay attention to the sounds you hear, both as a result of your steps and in the environment.

This activity requires your whole body and your full attention. If you notice your mind wandering as you walk, there is no need to judge or criticize it. It is your mind doing exactly what it was created to do. Refocus on the experience of walking.

Observe your thoughts

Another way to practice mindfulness is to observe your thoughts and differentiate them from yourself: "Observe," but don't get involved. You don't need to follow your thoughts, see where they go or interact with them. Just notice the judgments, anxieties, daydreams, and plans as they happen. If a thought triggers an emotion, register that it has occurred, don't get involved, and watch it disappear.

Finding objectivity takes power away from thoughts and emotions, allowing them to simply be a function of your mind. They are not under control. Practice this method of mindfulness regularly, preferably when you are calm. If emotions are intense and thoughts are racing, it may be important to practice one of the more guiding exercises first.

Repetition of affirmations

In practicing differentiating between self and thoughts and emotions, you can also choose carefully what you think about. If you have a choice, it may be helpful to choose something positive. In mindful dialogue, people are invited to think before they speak: Is it true, is it helpful, is it inspiring, is it necessary, and is it kind?

If you notice self-deprecating or distrustful thoughts being repeated, try choosing encouraging, uplifting, and rational thoughts. Select a mantra or affirmation such as, "I can choose to be kind to myself (and others)." Repeat it silently (or out loud). By doing so, you will not only reinforce its meaning but also provide yourself with an anchor that will help you overcome a moment of insecurity.

Benefits of mindfulness for BPD symptoms
The first benefit of mindfulness for BPD is that it is free. It also combines well with other wellness efforts. In addition, it can be practiced anywhere, anytime. However, reading about mindfulness is not enough to build a solid foundation. Fortunately, there are meditation apps and videos on the Internet to help you learn.

In addition, practicing mindfulness can produce immediate improvements. When you take intentional deep breaths or notice your senses, you can physically feel your body calm down. It is important to remember that the long-term benefits of mindfulness take time. Mindfulness will not make BPD go away, but it can help make it more manageable.

Take a deep breath, feel your thoughts slow down, and invest your attention in the experience of breathing. Consider using mindfulness beyond therapy for BPD or for general mental health maintenance. If you are curious, consider doing guided meditations and/or seeking out a mental health professional.

Chapter 4

Developing Healthy Relationships

Even after you have sought treatment for Borderline Personality Disorder (BPD), you may find maintaining personal relationships a difficult task. Why? To have received a diagnosis of BPD, it is likely that your symptoms were affecting various aspects of your life, particularly your relationships. The hallmarks of the disorder are intense emotional outbursts, mood instability, impulsivity, and anger can wreak havoc on your relationships. These aspects can make you feel powerless as if you have no chance of maintaining healthy relationships with others.

This is not true. You can have deep and meaningful relationships with your family, your friends, and your partner.

The widespread stereotypes and stigmas associated with Borderline Personality Disorder are often passed on to friends and loved ones. They hear that people with BPD are manipulative, suicidal, and angry, and these characteristics influence them to keep their distance. It might be difficult to have loved ones turn away from you due to your disorder. Here are some tips that can help your relationships during and after treatment:

Inform your friends and family. It is very important that the people around you have a good understanding of BPD and how it affects you. Encourage them to read books, brochures and watch documentaries about BPD. It may take some time for them to understand it clearly, but don't stop doing it. The best way for them to love you better is for them to understand you better.

If it's feasible, urge them to join you in treatment or support groups. Participating in your treatment is a great way to show support and help you improve your condition.

Explain to them that most behaviors are not deliberate as loved ones can easily be hurt by angry outbursts or exploitative behaviors. People around you must learn not to take these behaviors personally. One of the main aspects of BPD is emotional immaturity. Their behaviors are a reflection of an illness. Family and friends need to see these behaviors as constructs of the illness, not you.

Expect it to take time. Give your loved ones some space to digest the diagnosis and take care of themselves so they can be in the best position to take care of you. The OPI Intensive for young men and women offers you the opportunity to get better in a safe and nurturing environment. In addition to working on your current relationships, you will also work on building new relationships with others.

Your loved ones need to be patient with you during the treatment process; however, you also need to realize that they are suffering as well. Make every effort to give your loved ones the opportunity to participate or be informed of your progress at the residential treatment center for Borderline Personality Disorder (BPD). By working together, you can build stronger and healthier relationships for the future.

Open communication and stronger, more stable relationships go a long way in your attempt to overcome borderline personality disorder. But, healthy relationships and BPD healing might be hampered by uncontrollable emotions.

Communication Strategies for Setting Healthy Boundaries

Effective communication can be challenging for anybody, but it can be particularly challenging for those who suffer from borderline personality disorder. It can be quite irritating to feel as though no matter how you describe yourself, no one really gets it. It can be simpler to communicate your demands and ideas and to be understood if you have basic communication skills.

Focus

It is important to focus on the issue at hand as there is a tendency to bring up past issues to defend or accuse, but this should be avoided. Bringing up the past only confuses and distracts from the issue at hand. Remember that the past cannot be changed, so bringing it up only adds fuel to a potentially combative discussion.

Trust

For communication to be effective, there must be a general level of trust between the parties, especially in personal and intimate relationships. In general, the more intimate the relationship, the higher the level of trust needed. For example, if you don't trust your partner, you won't be able to be vulnerable, convey your disappointment, or ask for things from your significant other. Trust is essential to maintaining a meaningful dialogue.

Breathe

Breathing is something you should always remember to do during talks, especially challenging conversations. During an emotional or confrontational discussion, you may find yourself holding your breath or feeling your way through, which can aggravate your feelings of anger and frustration. Taking slow, deep breaths is one way to hold negative emotions and communicate more clearly.

Listen

During an argument, truly listening can be very difficult. Many people wait for their moment to speak. Effective communication requires paying close attention to what the other person is saying, even if it is something you disagree with.
Listening and repeating what you have heard is the best way to make sure you have really "heard" what the other person is saying.

Understand

Even if you don't agree with what the other person is saying, it is helpful to try to understand their point of view. You are just taking the first step toward good communication and resolution when you comprehend the other person's perspective. You cannot communicate your point of view without understanding the other person's point of view.

"I" Statements

"I's" are among the most effective language techniques. If used correctly, they remove any accusatory tone from the statement and allow you to express your point of view without eliciting a defensive reaction. *The 3 important parts of an "I-statement":*

- *State your feeling*
- *Linking the feeling to a problem*
- *Saying what you want to happen*

"When you make decisions without asking or informing me, I feel left out," for example, is a more appropriate statement to make using the "I-statement" technique than "You never include me in decisions." I would like for us to get together often so that we may discuss our choices and make decisions."

Take a break

Sometimes it's important to pause and not continue the conversation. The pause gives everyone a chance to take perspective, step back from negative feelings, and think about the real purpose of the conversation and how to proceed. Too often, people start talking about a topic that triggers negative thoughts or feelings, which leads them to start talking about another topic. People also spend a lot of time looking for a solution to an argument when one is not possible. Pausing gives you permission to stop the conversation once the topic has been clarified.

Don't focus on winning

People often focus on winning or being right, which usually means they are asking the other person to admit they were wrong. When people focus on winning, others tend to feel that their feelings or perspectives are ignored or disrespected. This will only lead to defensiveness and escalation on both sides. Instead, focus on understanding different points of view.

Know your objective

When you are arguing with someone, it is important to know what the objective of the communication is. If the objective is something you don't control, the communication will be frustrating and useless. Often, the whole purpose of expressing your emotions is to give your thoughts a voice. It is the other person's responsibility to choose to act if they want to help you feel better.

Admit Responsibility

We all make mistakes. Sometimes we even hurt those we love the most. Allow yourself to acknowledge and admit the less admirable things you do. If you have hurt someone, even if unintentionally, acknowledge what you have done and apologize. Once responsibility is taken, real communication can begin. It's critical to keep in mind that doing wrong or injuring someone does not define you as a "bad" person. However, you must also remember that the person you have hurt does not stop feeling bad just because you have apologized.

Chapter 5

Mastering Self-Identity and Self-Esteem

Boosting self-esteem is an essential ingredient for coping with a mental health diagnosis, overcoming an addiction, or simply having the life you want to lead. If you embark on a journey to improve your self-esteem, you'll find that everything in life gets better along the way.

However, this path calls for patience with others as much as with oneself. If some of your closest friends have always thought poorly of you, you could be startled if they don't respond well to your newfound self-worth.

Along the way, you may begin to question whether you really deserve to have self-esteem. This is natural. Know that you have made the decision to improve your life and that you will reap the benefits of that decision.

Here are some simple ways to get started on the road to a better version of yourself:

Remember compliments: in a compliment journal - Write down nice things people have said or done to you in a journal you keep handy. Refer to it when you're having a bad day.

Focus on positive qualities: We all have less attractive traits, so concentrate on your favorable attributes. Consider your whole net worth as positive rather than negative. Create a list of your strengths and have it close at hand.

Listen to the voice inside your head: If tells you something like, "You're going to blow this presentation," respond to it with deliberate affirmations such, "I've worked hard and have confidence and prepared." The way you say to yourself can have a significant impact on your emotional state.

Acknowledge others: Recognize that everyone around you cares about your self-esteem as much as you do. Stop, listen, and pay attention to the people you interact with. Making them feel acknowledged will make you feel like you've done something good.

Discover how to express your desires without feeling bad about it: Never hesitate to communicate your demands to others, whether it's by asking a family member to make supper or informing your boss that you must arrive at work later than usual in order to escape traffic. People can be surprisingly accommodating when you ask nicely and clearly. Fulfilling your life's necessities can significantly boost your self-worth.

Maintain a record of your accomplishments and objectives by writing down one item you accomplished each day, even if it was only remembering to work out, and one aspiration you have for the following day. Your brain will assess your accomplishments and motivate you to keep pursuing your objectives.

Get Past Your Own Stigmatization

At times, the worst stigma that people encounter originates from within.

Individuals with borderline personality disorder (BPD) may experience symptoms as a direct result of their inability to accept who they are or their uneasiness in relationships. Regretfully, a lot of individuals with BPD also think they are unworthy of other people's love and respect or that they are unworthy of anything.

In addition to making it harder for them to get along with others, people with BPD who do not accept who they are may also engage in self-sabotaging behaviors that prevent them from achieving significant goals in their academic or professional lives. Feelings of self-hatred may also result from this lack of acceptance of oneself. Unable to accept who they are, people with BPD may be more likely to self-harm or even attempt suicide. It's also typical for BPD sufferers who struggle more with self-acceptance to have feelings of loneliness or isolation.

Becoming accepting of oneself is crucial to BPD healing. People will react favorably to you when you respect and love yourself.

Here are some tips for raising self-acceptance:

Seek out expert assistance

It's quite acceptable to look for expert assistance. Speak with a therapist who is covered by your insurance. They can assist you in accurately diagnosing yourself and discussing your journey towards self-acceptance. Don't be afraid to talk to your therapist about your diagnosis if you have one already. Recognize the range of skills that various experts possess.

Locate a creative outlet

Having a creative outlet helps a lot of people deal with their emotions and provides solace. To explore your feelings, you can write, draw, paint, knit, play music, dance, sing, sculpt, and keep an art journal. As you progress, you'll eventually grow to have a good sense of satisfaction or pride. The path to self-acceptance and self-love is paved with these feelings.

Recognize your shortcomings

Everyone, including you, is flawed. It's acceptable to be imperfect and make mistakes. It's what gives you your humanity. It's another quality that sets you apart. If everyone was flawless, there would be no interest. Failures and mistakes can provide valuable learning opportunities. You probably know someone who has accomplished remarkable things despite facing many challenges. These setbacks can also heighten the significance of our victories. Self-compassion practice can be helpful for a lot of individuals.

Create a safety net

People who struggle with self-acceptance require a network of support to assist them in getting better when they're feeling low. Right now, you most likely have a fantastic support network within your own environment. When you need a little encouragement, talk to your parents, grandparents, siblings, and friends. Naturally, you must remember to assist them as well as necessary.

Of course, a lot of people lack a family that is encouraging or affirming. It only indicates that they are a dysfunctional family and are unable to provide for you. Thankfully, there are different choices. Discuss support groups and other mental health options with your therapist. Meeting others in the support group could make it easier to create a network of support. Once more, remember to give back the favors you receive.

Emphasize physical well-being
You'll feel better on the inside when you're feeling good about yourself. Those who despise themselves occasionally overindulge in processed, high-calorie foods.

Rather, attend to your bodily well-being. Eating properly means choosing to eat more fruits and vegetables. There's no shortage of evidence supporting the very positive effects of physical activity. You'll be astonished at how much your mental state can improve by putting your physical health first.

Say encouraging words aloud
Positive affirmations are brief statements that you can repeat to yourself or in the mirror to support yourself when you need a little pick-me-up during the day. You can categorize these affirmations into groups like "can-do affirmations" and "beauty affirmations." Go through the beauty affirmations whenever you need to feel good about your appearance. These ought to be a summary of your greatest qualities and basic statements regarding beauty. Read the "can do" affirmations whenever you need encouragement to be there for friends and family or support at work.

Decide to pardon

People frequently carry past traumas for years at a time. On an emotional level, this trauma can make things much heavier than they need to be. In order to release yourself from the burden of that trauma, you must learn to forgive others. You have the ability to forgive those who have wronged you, whether they are parents or long-time friends. This does not imply that you will no longer feel the hurt or the fallout from those choices.

Assist others

You will find that focusing your attention on those in need of your assistance for several hours each week will help you accept who you are. Help others with your time. You could start by going to see your loved ones. Another option is to become active with a charity. Upon completion of the task, your self-esteem will improve.

Concentrate on making tiny gains.

Many desire to witness significant advancements quickly. In all honesty, you won't notice much improvement at first. You must practice patience and pay attention to tiny victories. Start with a modest objective, like rising a little earlier each day, working out most days, maintaining a healthy diet, or spending time with family or friends once a weekend. Once you've completed the initial step, set a new, marginally more difficult objective. You will eventually begin to experience times when you love and accept who you are. You'll feel accomplished when you consider who you were a year or two ago. Pursue advancement over perfection.

Chapter 6

Handling Self-Injury and Suicidal Thoughts

It's critical to understand how to manage suicidal thoughts in the context of borderline personality disorder (BPD). Keep in mind that you don't have to handle BPD thoughts alone. Locating safe havens where you can freely and safely express these emotions when they surface is crucial.

When you keep them to yourself, they become threatening and solitary. Support can come from confidants or a trusted spiritual advisor, group therapy, a support group of some kind, supportive family, and friends. It also entails knowing to whom you can confide these thoughts. Not everyone is ready or aware of how to respond appropriately when they are having such thoughts. Even though this may hurt, you will discover along the journey who is capable of supporting you during your difficult times and knowing how to react in a way that is appropriate and healthy. When in trouble, it can be more detrimental to turn to unhelpful people than beneficial. It's not that they don't care about you; rather, it's that they lack the knowledge necessary to support you in those circumstances.

It's also critical to acknowledge that the coping and self-calming strategies that follow might not always be sufficient. It's critical to understand who you are and to realize when you pose a risk to yourself.

These thoughts typically result from intense emotional outbursts or feelings of abandonment in most people. Even if, deep down, they only want to let go of or escape their suffering rather than believing they want to die.

Here are a few strategies for it:

Speak with a different BPD friend: Nobody understands this suffering better than a peer who has been diagnosed with BPD or another severe mental illness.

Calm down and divert: Taking an ice cube and gripping it tightly until it melts is an illustration of a divert strategy.

Loud music: Dancing until the urges subside while listening to loud music in the living room can occasionally be beneficial.

Take a bath: Unwinding in a bathtub filled with essential oils will assist you in coming back to your physical self and calming down.

Engage in spiritual activities: When such feelings occur, meditating is actually the worst thing you could do. However, it is very beneficial to walk while praying, stay physically active, and establish a strong connection with a deep source of love.

Journaling: Record your feelings of rage, self-loathing, and suicidal ideas. Try writing substitute thoughts in its place. In case you write something like, "These feelings are going to kill me." Saying to yourself, "This is very difficult right now, but it too will pass," is a healthy coping mechanism. I've experienced this before, but I overcame it."

Spend time with a pet: Bathing your pet is one of your other favorite activities. As absurd as it may seem, your pet can provide a great deal of solace and tranquility. Occasionally, taking care of it diverts your attention just enough to dull the emotions.

Spend the night with a friend or relative: When we experience troubling thoughts, we sometimes can't handle being by ourselves. It can be a lot less frightening to know that you have company. It also helps a lot to confide in a close friend, spend time with them, and avoid being alone.

Call the nearest emergency room, the local police, or 911 if you're in the US or Canada, if you or someone you know is in immediate danger of taking their own life.

If you are not in immediate danger, but you are having such thoughts and need support, call a helpline to talk about your feelings and find local resources. You can call the National Suicide Prevention Lifeline if you are in the US. It is available twenty-four hours a day, seven days a week, and is free and private.

Chapter 7

Getting Over BPD

Many believe that receiving a diagnosis of "mental illness" is detrimental. In actuality, the diagnosis conceals a complete person with innate creativity, empathy, a profound love of life, and limitless potential.

The public, mental health professionals and the media stigmatize BPD beyond recognition. Many internet resources perpetuate misconceptions about BPD by emphasizing its negative aspects. People lose sight of the person behind the label and the possible advantages of BPD when they exclusively concentrate on the negative symptoms.
However, there is a distinct person with their own strengths, resiliency, and positive traits hiding behind the BPD label. If we only pay attention to the negative symptoms, we run the risk of undervaluing the individual and ignoring their potential for development and constructive contributions.

Many BPD sufferers are perceptive, deep thinkers, and gifted intellectuals. Contrary to popular assumption, the majority of BPD sufferers are highly self-aware and introspective. They can become the most compassionate and forward-thinking leaders through a process of healing and transformation.

They have a great sense of empathy
The remarkable capacity of people with borderline personality disorder to fully comprehend and empathize with the emotional experiences of others is one of the disorder's most notable benefits.

In fact, when an emotional storm hits, you might momentarily lose perspective or behave strangely. Some people might mistake your nature and claim that you lack empathy because of your chaotic attachment style, push-pull pattern, and relational difficulties. But this is a false and unfair presumption. Many BPD sufferers describe themselves as "empaths." An empath is a person who is so empathetic that they experience other people's pain as though it were their own; occasionally, they are unable to distinguish between their own feelings and those of others.

This can be explained by a number of psychological theories, including the overactivity of his mirror neurons, specific hormones in his physiology, abnormal brain wiring, or a turbulent upbringing where he was "trained" to be hypervigilant and may have needed to recognize early warning signs of his parents' anger to protect himself and his siblings.

In addition, he has a profound understanding of what it means to suffer because of his own experience with emotional pain. Because of this comprehension, he is able to assist and console individuals who are depressed, worried, or grieving. His silent understanding of their struggles and profound empathy is communicated through his presence without words. From a psychological standpoint, it can be immensely consoling to simply be with someone who shares your pain. They feel validated when they can relate to you emotionally and can truly see and understand your inner turmoil.

Sufferers understand that you understand them spiritually. They take solace in the knowledge that you are aware of the intricacy of their internal struggles when they are at their lowest. This acknowledgment can provide a ray of hope and a reminder that they are not traveling alone, fostering a strong sense of connection and shared humanity.

Honoring and appreciating this gift of understanding is crucial because it enables you to serve as a lighthouse of empathy and encouragement for others. But you also have to look after yourself and establish sensible limits. Sometimes the weight of another person's suffering can be too much to bear, and in order to preserve emotional health, it's critical to know when to set boundaries.

Incredibly observant

The capacity to see past outward interactions and pick up on minute shifts in mood and emotion is one of the disorder's unexpected benefits.

In fact, studies indicate that compared to those without BPD, those with BPD frequently have a higher capacity for recognizing subtle mood swings and facial expressions. Because of their improved perception, people with BPD and their friends have made many jokes about their "psychic abilities."

On the one hand, being able to recognize subliminal dynamics and uncover hidden emotions can be highly advantageous. It enables you to comprehend the genuine intentions of those around you and to perform better in social situations. Your ability to perceive things clearly can also help you succeed in both your personal and professional life because it will enable you to make intuitive decisions and insightful observations.

But this gift also comes with difficulties. Being able to spot dishonesty, injustice, and deception can make your life more difficult because you might find it hard to put up with or overlook such actions. Seeing the contradiction between people's words and deeds time and time again can be depressing and add to your frustration in your never-ending quest for justice and authenticity.

Additionally, people who prefer not to be seen or held accountable for their actions may feel threatened or uneasy due to their perceptive nature. It may take deliberate effort, good judgment, and some mentalization skills to strike a balance between following your gut and not overreacting to your overactive mirror neurons, as well as between utilizing your intuition and honoring other people's boundaries. Put differently, you need to work on transitioning from "emotional empathy" to "cognitive empathy." It may take some time and practice to develop the skills necessary to effectively and constructively communicate your observations without inadvertently hurting or alienating others, but doing so will enable you to harness your innate instincts and turn them into strengths.

But if you can learn to use your intuition carefully and skillfully, it can become a very useful tool that can help you succeed both personally and professionally. Your capacity to see beyond appearances, foresee needs, and comprehend the unsaid can help you develop stronger interpersonal relationships, improve your problem-solving abilities, and move through challenging circumstances with poise and wisdom.

Keep in mind that you should value your perceptiveness and try to use it to your advantage by developing mindset skills along the way. Finding a balance between attending to other people's feelings and taking care of your own needs is also crucial. By establishing boundaries, developing self-awareness, keeping your emotional equilibrium, and asking for help when you need it, you can harness the power of your intuition.

You might go unnoticed by others.
Despite the fact that others might not always see or understand you, people with borderline personality disorder are nevertheless capable of showing compassion and love. There is a remarkably sensitive heart hidden behind the emotional chaos and extreme mood fluctuations. Being in love with someone who has BPD is a profound and all-encompassing experience; it is neither transient nor superficial.

A person with borderline personality disorder truly loves. They are completely devoted to each other. They welcome the intensity and vulnerability that come with being totally present in their relationships. They display sincere concern and affection for their loved ones, don't hesitate to communicate their emotions, and frequently wear their hearts on their sleeves.

Love is often experienced by a person with BPD in a way that defies categorization. They understand what it means to be unusual, so they know how to value each person's individuality. They frequently possess the ability to see past appearances, establish soulful connections with people, and recognize the beauty that resides within them.

They also don't take anything for granted because they were denied everything when they were young. As a result, they are able to recognize and value their partners' silent words, small gestures, and subtle nuances that others might miss.

In fact, fear and insecurity can coexist with love for someone who has borderline personality disorder (BPD). Having a fear of being rejected or abandoned can make it difficult to keep stable, healthy relationships going. But in spite of these challenges, people with BPD exhibit true, profound love.

Loving someone who has BPD is also a special experience. Because they have gone through emotional disorders themselves, these people have an innate ability to understand and empathize with the suffering and struggles of others. Because of their empathy, they are able to provide their loved ones with unmatched care and support during difficult times.

You can reap the many benefits of Borderline Personality Disorder together by acknowledging and appreciating the sincerity and depth of those who are experiencing emotional storms. However, loving someone who is experiencing emotional turmoil of their own presents special challenges. Others can appreciate the beauty of your love and forge enduring relationships with you if you are able to manage and comprehend your emotions.

In summary, people with BPD are capable of intense, passionate, and unconditional love—even though others might not always be able to recognize it. Their love is proof of their tenacity, fortitude, and the enormous potential of the human heart.

Utilizing borderline personality disorder's benefits in artistic endeavors
Many BPD sufferers express their suffering through art, poetry, music, or other mediums. Throughout history, exceptionally gifted and talented writers, actors, and artists have given meaning to their existential anxiety and mental pain.

BPD patients can experience extremely intense pain that frequently defies verbal expression. During these moments, the arts can serve as a potent conduit for your soul to express itself. You regain your power and refuse to be limited by victimhood by connecting with your creative essence and expressing your innermost struggles through artistic mediums.

You open your heart to the outside world through your creative expression. You can serve as a source of empathy and connection for people going through similar experiences by sharing your artistic creations. It is consoling to know that someone is out there, waiting to be reassured that they are not alone in their suffering and that there is someone else who can actually relate to and understand their situation.

You start a path of inspiration when you use creative outlets to find a language for your feelings. Your work becomes a bridge that can awaken the depths of human experience and evoke strong emotions. You can create communities—even if they are only virtual ones—by fearlessly sharing your works and touching people's hearts.

You are aware of what invisible trauma looks like
The benefits of having borderline personality disorder can include having an original perspective on life, which enables one to question social norms and promote social justice.

BPD is invisible, in contrast to a physical injury or disability. It is among the most excruciating illnesses a person can have, though. They might also have experienced emotional abuse or neglect as children, among other unseen traumas.

People with Borderline Personality Disorder (BPD) suffer a great deal, but this is often overlooked, especially if they seem to be doing well on the outside. But you are aware of the depth that can be concealed behind a façade. Your life experiences have imbued you with a profound empathy and comprehension of the intricacies of human emotions and challenges.

Many BPD sufferers are gifted activists who are fervent about the rights and perspectives of others. Their individual encounters with suffering and injustice may ignite a fervent desire to change the world for the better. Regardless of how it may be covered up or concealed, a profound awareness of the significance of acknowledging the suffering of every person drives much of this activist work.

People with BPD gain an understanding of other people's pain and a distinct perspective through their personal experience navigating the depths of emotional distress. They have personal experience with how social and structural factors affect mental health and overall well-being. Their fight for social justice, their efforts to give voice to the voiceless, and their establishment of inclusive and accepting spaces are all motivated by this knowledge.

People with BPD have the ability to truly impact others through their advocacy work, utilizing their personal experiences and empathetic qualities to empower and encourage others. They work to build a more understanding and compassionate society where everyone's experiences and voices are respected and valued by turning their pain into meaningful action. At that point, they use the advantages of having borderline personality disorder to give humanity—as well as themselves—a gift.

They find beauty in everything
They are deeply sensitive individuals who can sense and relate to the suffering that our world is experiencing as a whole. Although this sensitivity can occasionally be challenging, it also provides them with a profound appreciation for beauty. Love is not something you should take for granted, and even the smallest acts of kindness or displays of affection

can make you feel overwhelmed. A song's verse or a heartfelt gesture from a romantic partner are examples of the "little things" in life that can leave a profound and enduring impression.

They can perceive the world with a different vibration due to their heightened sensitivity, which enables them to vividly perceive the subtleties of ecstasy, deep love, and despair. It's crucial to understand that emotional sensitivity is a gift even though it can be difficult at times. It allows you to enter a world of depth and richness where you can have profoundly moving experiences of joy, wonder, and deep connection in ways that others might not fully comprehend.

Your ability to express yourself creatively and through writing, art, and other mediums can be enhanced by this sensitivity. You'll be able to find significance in the smallest details and recognize beauty in things that appear ordinary.

You have extraordinary resilience
One of the benefits of having borderline personality disorder is that it can help people become exceptionally resilient and adaptable when faced with obstacles in life.

BPD doesn't break you; instead, it molds you, makes you examine yourself, and fortifies you as a person.

You can flex under the weight of difficulties, just like a strong tree, but you don't allow them to break you. He has learned to appreciate how precious each day is as a result of the suffering and hopelessness he has endured.

Living with BPD reveals a wellspring of inner fortitude and resiliency. You become more resilient every day, evolving into a warrior who not only manages your BPD symptoms but also weathers the inevitable ups and downs that life will inevitably bring. You are now a stronger person as a result of your journey, able to handle adversity with determination and grace.

Your identity is much more complex than the fleeting changes brought on by mood swings. There's a part of you that will always be there, ready to welcome life in all its colorful complexity. Your determination to live, grow, and embrace who you truly are defines you even more than the difficulties you encounter.

Your experience has given you a distinct viewpoint that can uplift and support people going through difficult times.

Conclusion

Remind yourself to look after yourself as you continue to traverse the BPD landscape. Embrace self-compassion, ask for help when you need it, and acknowledge and celebrate all of your accomplishments, no matter how minor they may seem.

Accept your path as a fighter, confident in your ability to conquer every obstacle. Your inner self shines through surface fluctuations, determined to be alive and vibrant. Keep developing your resilience because you are an inspiration and a lighthouse for those who are on a similar journey.

Although accepting a diagnosis can be difficult, you shouldn't believe that your gifts will disappear simply because you have a diagnosis.
Finding methods to acknowledge and capitalize on your strengths is the next step. You might choose to write a song that recounts your life story or use your intense empathy to console a friend.

It hurts to be misinterpreted your entire life and is never acceptable. It is up to us to go from surviving to thriving, to not let the past haunt us, to stand up for our rights, and shine as vibrant human beings—even though we have no control over the opinions of others.

To move forward, you don't need your friends or family to understand you. It's not like you were helpless like it was when you were a kid. You have the right to turn away from those who are trying to gaslight or use you as a scapegoat. You will be shocked to learn how resilient you really are when you consider all the tragedies, murders, and broken relationships you have overcome. Despite the pressures of our society, walking away is difficult but necessary because you deserve it.

It's crucial to understand that a diagnosis does not sum up who you are. There's a huge part of your true self that's waiting to be found, beyond any diagnosis. Embracing the entirety of who you are and your journey of self-discovery is an amazing and powerful undertaking.

Remember to value and celebrate the characteristics that set you apart as you travel your path. Accept the benefits of having BPD, such as increased empathy, sensitivity, and emotional depth. These qualities can serve as wellsprings of fortitude, inventiveness, and interpersonal relationships.

I hope your path brings you to a complete comprehension and acceptance of who you are, independent of any classification or diagnosis. Accept your uniqueness, appreciate your distinctions, and never stop uncovering the depth and beauty that reside within you.

www.ingramcontent.com/pod-product-compliance
Lightning Source LLC
Chambersburg PA
CBHW071004260726
48661CB00007B/2790